Made in the USA
Las Vegas, NV
10 March 2022

45374230R00068